Date: 3/6/13

NATURE'S CHILDREN

TASMANIAN DEVILS

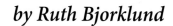

by Ruth Bjorklund

Children's Press®

An Imprint of Scholastic Inc.
New York Toronto London Auckland Sydney
Mexico City New Delhi Hong Kong
Danbury, Connecticut

Content Consultant
Dr. Stephen S. Ditchkoff
Professor of Wildlife Sciences
Auburn University
Auburn, Alabama

Photographs © 2013: age fotostock: 5 top, 15 (ARCO/Mosebach
K.), 11, 16 (Martin Zwick); Alamy Images: cover (Brian Elliott), 4, 5
background, 35 (Bruce Miller); Ardea/D. Parer & E. Parer-Cook/
Auscape: 24; Bob Italiano: 44 foreground, 45 foreground; Dreamstime/
Adrian Gabriel: 2 background, 3 background, 44 background, 45
background; Getty Images: 39, 40 (Adam Pretty), 36 (Brendon Thorne),
19 (Jason Edwards/National Geographic); Photo Researchers/Peter B.
Kaplan: 20; Reuters/Tim Wimborne: 23; Shutterstock, Inc.: 2 foreground,
3 foreground, 7 (Cloudia Newland), 12 (Patsy A. Jacks); Superstock, Inc.:
1, 5 bottom, 8, 46 (Animals Animals), 27, 28, 32 (NHPA); The Image
Works/The Natural History Museum: 31.

Library of Congress Cataloging-in-Publication Data
Bjorklund, Ruth.
  Tasmanian devils / by Ruth Bjorklund.
     pages cm.—(Nature's children)
  Includes bibliographical references and index.
  Audience: Ages 9–12.
  Audience: Grades 4–6.
  ISBN 978-0-531-20982-0 (lib. bdg.)
  ISBN 978-0-531-24308-4 (pbk.)
  1. Tasmanian devil—Juvenile literature. I. Title.
  QL737.M33B56 2013
  599.2'7—dc23   2012034332

All rights reserved. Published in 2013 by Children's Press, an imprint
of Scholastic Inc.
Printed in the United States of America 141
SCHOLASTIC, CHILDREN'S PRESS, and associated logos are
trademarks and/or registered trademarks of Scholastic Inc.

1 2 3 4 5 6 7 8 9 10 R 22 21 20 19 18 17 16 15 14 13

Tasmanian Devils

Class	Mammalia
Order	Dasyuromorphia
Family	Dasyuridae
Genus	*Sarcophilus*
Species	*Sarcophilus harrisii*
World distribution	Tasmania
Habitat	Forests, dense bush, grasslands, coastal areas, and mountains
Distinctive physical characteristics	Adult devils have black fur with a white stripe on the chest and sometimes white spots on sides and rump; large head with powerful jaws and sharp teeth; pointed pink ears; long, fat, bushy tail; females have a pouch to carry young
Habits	Devils are solitary, nocturnal hunters; when eating and confronted by other devils or predators, they make loud, aggressive barks and screams; attack with teeth and claws
Diet	Carrion makes up a significant portion of a devil's diet; will also hunt and kill snakes, birds, rodents, lizards, fish, and small mammals

Contents

CHAPTER 1

Creatures of the Night

It is night on the island of Tasmania. In the depths of the forest, several dark shapes are clustered together around the dead body of a wallaby. They are Tasmanian devils, feeding together on carrion. Suddenly, a bloodcurdling screech pierces the air. One of the smaller devils has gotten too close to a larger one. These animals may share food sometimes, but that doesn't make them friendly to one another. The larger devil opens its mouth wide to show off its pointed teeth. The smaller one slinks away in defeat, leaving the victorious devil to enjoy its meal.

The Tasmanian devil is the world's largest carnivorous marsupial. A marsupial is a mammal that has a pouch on its abdomen. Many of the world's marsupials, including kangaroos and koalas, live in Australia. The Tasmanian devil lives only in Tasmania, an island just south of mainland Australia.

Even as the world's largest carnivorous marsupials,
Tasmanian devils are fairly small animals.

Head to Tail

Tasmanian devils are strong and stocky. They have large heads, and their tails are nearly half as long as their bodies. An average Tasmanian devil measures 20 to 31 inches (51 to 79 centimeters) from nose to tail and stands about 12 inches (30 cm) tall. A well-fed Tasmanian devil can weigh up to 26 pounds (12 kilograms).

A devil's massive jaws hold 42 teeth, giving it one of the most powerful bites of any animal. Its ears glow pink in the sunlight because they have very little hair on them. The rest of its body is covered in black fur, except for a white stripe across its neck or white patches on its side or rump. The devil's long front legs and short rear legs cause it to walk unevenly, somewhat like a pig. Yet Tasmanian devils can climb trees, swim, and run up to 15 miles (24 kilometers) per hour.

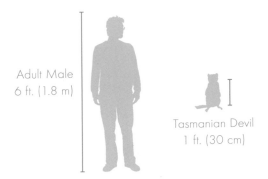

Adult Male
6 ft. (1.8 m)

Tasmanian Devil
1 ft. (30 cm)

Different devils have white patches on different parts of their bodies.

Night Hunters

Tasmanian devils are nocturnal. This means they hunt for food from dusk until dawn and sleep during the day. They scamper at speeds averaging 6 miles (10 km) per hour and cover 6 to 12 miles (10 to 19 km) every night. Tasmanian devils are scavengers. They usually eat dead animals because they are easy to acquire. If a devil cannot find carrion, however, it must kill a live animal. Devils are not quick, but they can chase and snap at their prey for several miles without getting tired.

Each devil hunts in its own home range, which extends from 1.5 to 10.4 square miles (4 to 27 square kilometers). Sometimes two devils meet while hunting in the same home range. They rarely attack each other, but they snarl and make threatening gestures before going their separate ways.

FUN FACT! Devils are sometimes called the "vacuum cleaners of the forest" because they eat carrion.

Carrion is a major part of a devil's diet.

CHAPTER 2

Rough and Tough

Adult Tasmanian devils are the top carnivores in Tasmania. This means that no other animals kill and eat them. Even so, devils are very protective of their food. Devils eat together, but they have very bad tempers when other devils get too close to them.

Devils lash out with frightening growls, shrieks, and unearthly screams. They bare their teeth and produce a foul-smelling odor when they are angry. Their ears turn bright red, and they claw and lunge at each other. The fierceness is really meant to scare others away, but if that fails, devils will attack. Many older devils have scarred faces and missing patches of fur from fighting with other angry devils.

*Tasmanian devils show off their fearsome teeth
when they want to frighten enemies away.*

The Senses

Tasmanian devils see mostly in black and white. While they are quite able to spot an animal moving in the darkness, their eyesight is not their strongest sense. Devils mainly rely on touch, hearing, and smell.

Devils have whiskers on their faces, chins, shoulders, and the top of their heads. The whiskers are sensitive to touch and help the devils find their prey in the dark. When eating alongside other devils, the whiskers help prevent them from getting too close to each other. Devils have excellent senses of hearing and smell. They raise their noses to sniff the air and turn their ears in the direction of a sound. That way, a devil can detect predators, prey, or another devil from far away.

Long whiskers help devils keep track of their surroundings.

Deep Sleep

Like other carnivorous marsupials such as quolls and dunnarts, Tasmanian devils conserve their energy by going into a state of torpor during the day. Their breathing rate and pulse slow, and they appear to be dead. Torpor resembles hibernation. But unlike a hibernating animal, a resting devil can spring in and out of torpor within seconds. In warmer months, devils use torpor to help them lower their body temperature.

In winter, when the weather is cold and food is scarce, devils will often spend the day basking in the sun. This helps them stay as warm as possible and lowers their need for food and water.

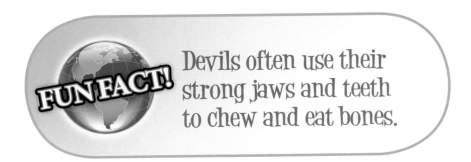

FUN FACT!

Devils often use their strong jaws and teeth to chew and eat bones.

Naps in the afternoon sunlight help keep devils warm and healthy in colder months.

Survival Skills

Tasmanian devils have many adaptations that help them survive in the wild. During the day, they have learned to protect themselves by hiding in caves, holes, and dense bush. They become active at night, hunting quietly while their dark fur keeps them hidden from view. Their white patches help make their shape harder for prey to recognize in the darkness. Devils use their short back legs and claws to climb trees to hunt for possums and birds or to escape from attack. Tasmanian devils also rely on their claws to dig holes, hunt for prey, fight one another, and eat.

Devils are good swimmers. In hot weather, devils seek out cool water to soak their bodies or to store their food for later meals. They put the food in the water and come back to eat it when they get hungry.

A Tasmanian devil's claws enable it to climb trees, dig holes, and fight.

CHAPTER 3

Island Home

The island of Tasmania is made up of a variety of habitats, including coastlines, mountains, rain forests, grasslands, and dry woodlands. Tasmanian devils like to dwell in dense vegetation. This helps them stay hidden from potential prey. Devils prefer wilderness areas along the coast and dry eucalyptus forests. Some devils also live near farms and towns.

Devils make their dens in hollow logs, wombat burrows, or small caves. Sometimes they seek shelter under a house or barn. Devils usually have three or four different dens. They can switch among them, depending on where they are when it comes time to go to sleep.

FUN FACT! Devils sometimes let loose a huge sneeze when they feel threatened.

Tasmanian devils make their dens wherever they can find a hidden space.

Eating Habits

Carrion is a major part of a Tasmanian devil's diet. Devils also eat reptiles, frogs, fish, rodents, insects, and small mammals. Their favorite prey animals are wombats and wallabies. Some Tasmanian devils kill chickens or eat the carcasses of livestock. Roadkill is another regular source of food.

Devils devour their food quickly. They can eat up to 40 percent of their body weight in 20 to 30 minutes. After eating, their bellies are so bloated that they must waddle off to rest and digest their meal.

The devil's diet helps the balance of nature on the island. Devils rid the forests of diseased, dead, and rotting animals. In farming areas, they stop the spread of insects and disease by eating livestock carcasses. When devils hunt prey, they kill the weakest animals they can find. This leaves the strongest to survive and breed. Devils also protect native species, especially birds, by hunting predators such as feral cats and non-native red foxes.

Devils sometimes challenge each other for freshly discovered carrion.

Breeding Season

Tasmanian devils mate in March. Their babies are born in April. Male devils fight each other to win a female. Then the successful male wrestles with the female to convince her to mate. For three weeks, the males guard the pregnant females to keep other males away. After the babies are born, the females attack and send their mates away. Tasmanian devils have more injuries from mating than from fighting over food.

Marsupials also have differences that set them apart from other mammals. They have a fold of skin called a pouch on their abdomen. Their babies are born very early and finish growing inside the mother's pouch.

Newborn devils live in their mother's pouch.

Tiny Devils

Tasmanian devils give birth after only 18 to 21 days. Baby devils are called joeys or sometimes imps. They are very tiny at first. Four baby devils could fit on a single quarter. They have no fur or ears and just tiny dots for eyes.

A female devil gives birth to 20 to 40 babies, but only the first four that climb into her pouch will survive. For about 100 days, the four joeys develop inside the mother's pouch and feed on her milk. When they emerge from the pouch, they are fully formed and weigh about 7 ounces (198 grams). For the next few months, they live in their mother's den. They are playful and very noisy. In the beginning, the mother hunts and brings food to the joeys. A few weeks later, the joeys go with her. By the time they are six months old, joeys are independent of their mother.

Joeys stay close to their mother for the first few months of their lives.

Growing Up

After joeys become independent, they are called juveniles. Nearly 1 out of 10 juveniles will not survive to adulthood. Although adult devils have no predators, juveniles have many. These predators include owls, eagles, foxes, and dogs. But more juveniles are eaten by adult devils than any other animals. Many juveniles try to avoid adult devils by being active during the day and hiding in dens at night.

Juveniles often escape predators by climbing trees. They are better climbers than adult devils. Juveniles spend most of their first year eating foods they find in trees. These foods include grubs, insects, eggs, and small birds. When they are strong enough, they begin to hunt on the ground and join carrion feasts.

Juvenile devils must be careful to avoid predators.

CHAPTER 4

A Rugged Past

Australia was once part of a larger landmass. Animals roamed freely throughout it. But 65 million years ago, Australia broke away and drifted toward the equator and the southern oceans. The temperature changed, and the continent turned hot during the day and cold at night.

In 1980, scientists discovered a series of caves in a limestone deposit in northwestern Australia. In the caves were 30 million-year-old fossils belonging to hundreds of Australian plant and animal species. Included among them were the ancestors of the Tasmanian devil.

At another historical site, scientists unearthed a skeleton of a man thought to be at least 7,000 years old. Around his neck was a necklace made of 178 Tasmanian devil teeth. Experts believe the teeth were important symbols to early humans in Australia.

Remains such as this jawbone have helped scientists learn about the history of Tasmanian devils.

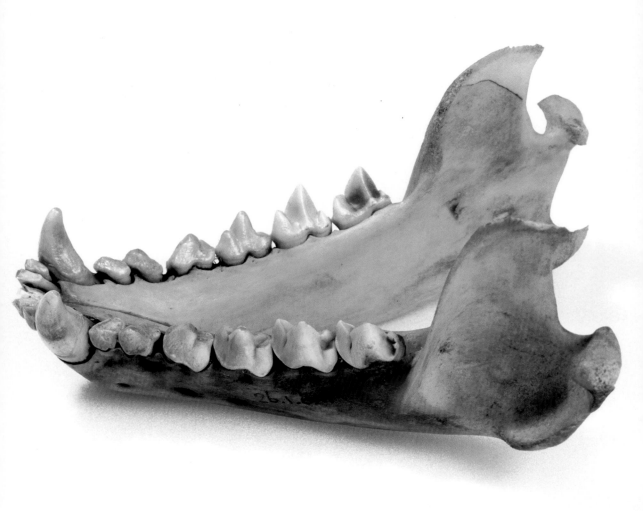

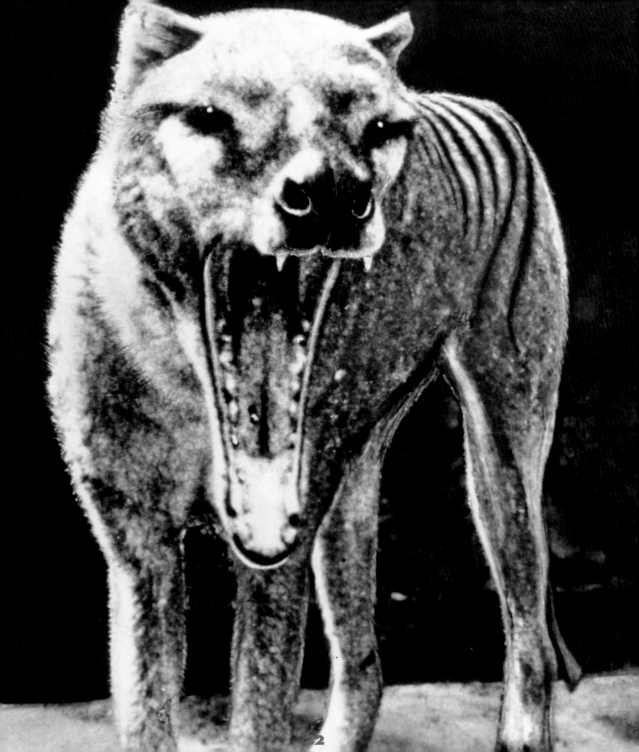

A New Home

Scientists say the first Tasmanian devils were tree dwellers. Their short legs developed to help them move from branch to branch. Living in trees, they were protected from predators. Devils eventually joined their closest relative, the quoll, in hunting for food on the ground. But the devils became prey for wild dogs called dingoes. Many scientists believe that the devil's nasty behavior is a result of its ancestors' need to fend off dingoes.

Around 400 to 600 years ago, devils disappeared from mainland Australia. They continued to survive on nearby Tasmania, however, and the dingoes did not. A large marsupial called the Tasmanian tiger became the devil's main predator. Seventy years ago, Tasmanian tigers became extinct. This made the Tasmanian devil the largest surviving meat-eating marsupial.

Tasmanian tigers were not actual tigers, but rather a type of large carnivorous marsupial.

CHAPTER 5

Fighting for Their Lives

The first European settlers in Tasmania were groups of British prisoners and their guards. In 1803, a group settled in the capital city of Hobart. At night, the newcomers heard terrifying screams coming from the forest. They called the creature "the devil" long before they saw one face-to-face.

The settlers declared war on the devils. They wrongly believed the devils preyed on their livestock and attacked humans. Guards trapped the devils and fed them to the prisoners. In the 1930s, a bounty was put on the devils. Anyone who trapped or poisoned a devil was paid 25 cents for a male and 35 cents for a female. The devils nearly became extinct. In 1941, the Tasmanian government passed laws protecting the devil. These laws helped the devil population to recover, but have not saved them completely.

Early European settlers in Tasmania were frightened by the devil's screaming sounds.

Devils and Humans

Today, the Tasmanian devil is on the world's threatened and endangered species list. This means that it could soon become extinct if nothing is done to help it survive.

Humans have destroyed the devil's natural habitat in many ways, such as by logging and clearing land for farming. Wilderness areas are also damaged by air and water pollution.

Highways and roads are dangerous for devils. Many animals are struck by cars and trucks. At night, devils come out to eat the roadkill. Nighttime drivers do not see the devils until it is too late.

Many devils, looking for food, live near farms and make their dens under houses and barns. They steal blankets and clothing to line their dens. Devils are smelly and are not welcome. Most farmers insist that devils attack their livestock, though experts believe that this happens only rarely. Hundreds of devils are trapped or poisoned by farmers every year.

The devil's taste for carrion often draws it toward streets and highways, where roadkill is plentiful.

Deadly Disease

Since the 1990s, a mysterious cancer has been killing devils by the thousands. It is called Devil Facial Tumor Disease (DFTD). Tumors form on the head and neck and can kill the devils in six months' time. The sickness can be passed from one devil to another.

Scientists have been working tirelessly to find the cause and a cure. Animal researchers have tried various treatments. So far, no medicine has helped to prevent or cure the disease. They are also studying the devil's **genes** for clues about how the disease first began to spread. Scientists have traced the start of the disease back to a single female. All the devils that have developed the disease are in some way related to her. Scientists hope that further genetic studies will help them find a way to stop the spread of DFTD.

Devil facial tumor disease is a major problem for devils today.

Rescue Plans

Without a cure in sight, many people are looking for other ways of saving the devil. Scientists are tracking healthy devils in the rain forest. They hope to find out what keeps them free of DFTD. The Australia Zoo and the Save the Tasmanian Devil Program capture healthy devils and raise them in captivity.

Some devils are sheltered in areas similar to their natural environment. One project on the Australian mainland, called Devil Ark, has 500 healthy devils living in a disease-free area. In Tasmania, scientists are breeding devils in a remote mountain wilderness. There are plans to relocate healthy devils to other parts of Tasmania, including some small islands off the coast. Countless volunteers help care for the devils and raise money for rescue programs.

Tasmanians are proud of their devils. They are devoted to finding a way to save one of the world's most famous and unusual creatures.

Scientists hope that their efforts will one day put an end to DFTD.

Words to Know

abdomen (AB-duh-men) — the part of the body between the chest and the hips

adaptations (ad-ap-TAY-shuhnz) — changes that living things go through so they can fit in better with their environments

ancestors (AN-ses-turz) — ancient animal species that are related to modern species

basking (BASK-ing) — lying or sitting in the sun

bounty (BOUN-tee) — a reward offered for the capture of an animal

captivity (kap-TIV-i-tee) — the condition of being held or trapped by people

carnivorous (kar-NIV-ur-uhs) — having meat as a regular part of the diet

carrion (KAR-ee-uhn) — dead animal flesh

dens (DENZ) — the homes of wild animals

endangered (en-DAYN-jurd) — at risk of becoming extinct, usually because of human activity

extinct (ik-STINGKT) — no longer found alive

feral (FAIR-ul) — domestic species that are now living in wild populations

fossils (FOSS-uhlz) — the hardened remains of prehistoric plants and animals

genes (JEENZ) — chemical codes in the body that pass traits from a parent to its offspring

habitats (HAB-uh-tats) — the places where an animal or a plant is usually found

home range (HOME RAYNJ) — area of land in which animals spend most of their time

juveniles (JOO-vuh-nuhlz) — animals that are neither babies nor adults

mammal (MAM-uhl) — a warm-blooded animal that has hair or fur and usually gives birth to live young

marsupial (mar-SOO-pee-uhl) — a mammal that has a pouch on the abdomen that is used to nourish and carry the young

mate (MAYT) — to join together to produce babies

nocturnal (nahk-TUR-nuhl) — active mainly at night

pollution (puh-LOO-shuhn) — harmful materials that damage or contaminate the air, water, and soil

predators (PREH-duh-turz) — animals that live by hunting other animals for food

prey (PRAY) — an animal that is hunted by another animal for food

scavengers (SKAV-en-jurz) — animals that feed on dead animals

species (SPEE-sheez) — one of the groups into which animals and plants of the same genus are divided

torpor (TOR-pur) — a short-term decrease in activity that is similar to hibernation

Habitat Map

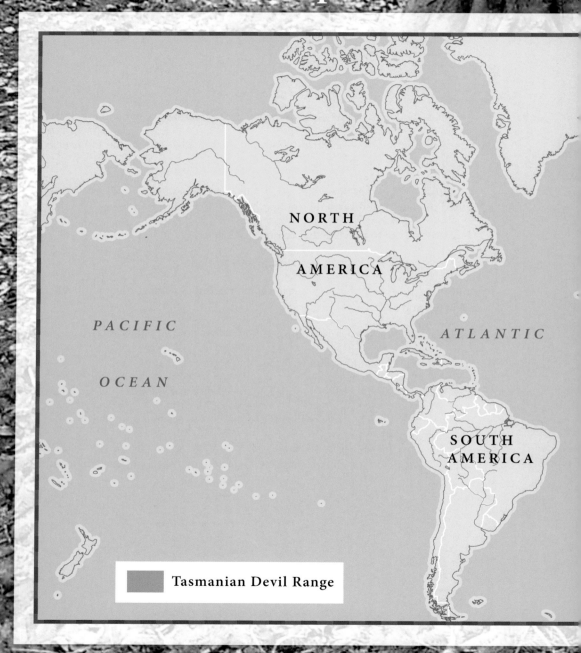

NORTH

AMERICA

PACIFIC

OCEAN

ATLANTIC

SOUTH
AMERICA

Tasmanian Devil Range

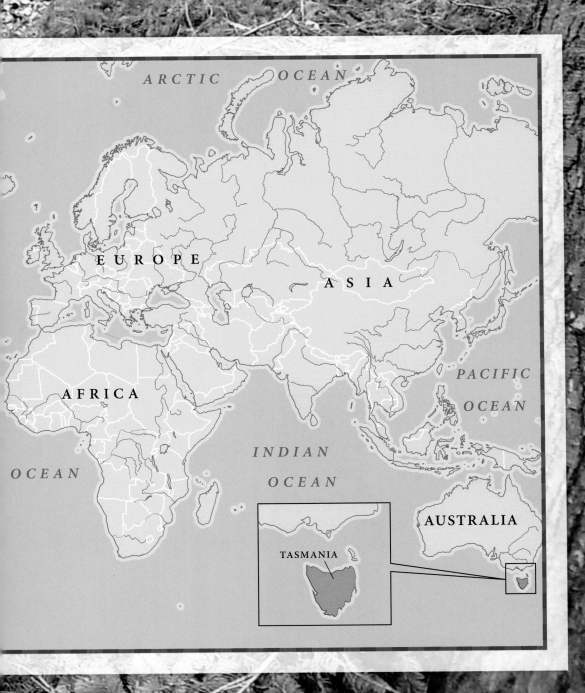

ARCTIC OCEAN

EUROPE

ASIA

AFRICA

PACIFIC OCEAN

INDIAN OCEAN

OCEAN

AUSTRALIA

TASMANIA

Find Out More

Books

Markle, Sandra. *Tasmanian Devils*. Minneapolis: Lerner Publications, 2005.

Markovics, Joyce L. *Tasmanian Devil: Nighttime Scavenger*. New York: Bearport Publishing, 2009.

Portman, Michael. *Tasmanian Devils in Danger*. New York: Gareth Stevens, 2012.

Visit this Scholastic Web site for more information on tasmanian devils:
www.factsfornow.scholastic.com
Enter the keywords **Tasmanian Devils**

Index

Page numbers in *italics* indicate a photograph or map.

About the Author

Ruth Bjorklund lives on Bainbridge Island in Washington State. She graduated with a master's degree in library and information science from the University of Washington in Seattle. She has written numerous books for young people, many of them about animals, including endangered species. She hopes that readers will join her in sending thoughts of encouragement to the many rescuers active in saving the Tasmanian devil from extinction.